BRING ME THE HEAD OF WILLY THE MAILBOY!

A DILBERT® BOOK BY SCOTT ADAMS

Andrews and McMeel
A Universal Press Syndicate Company
Kansas City

Other Dilbert Books from Andrews and McMeel

Shave the Whales
ISBN: 0-8362-1740-3, $8.95

Dogbert's Clues for the Clueless
ISBN: 0-8362-1737-3, $7.95

Build a Better Life by Stealing Office Supplies
ISBN: 0-8362-1757-8, $7.95

Always Postpone Meetings with Time-Wasting Morons
ISBN: 0-8362-1758-6, $7.95

For ordering information, call 1-800-642-6480

Dogbert and Dilbert appear in the comic strip Dilbert®, distributed by United Feature Syndicate, Inc.

ISBN: 0-8362-1779-9

Library of Congress Catalog Card Number: 94-73226

First Printing, March 1995
Second Printing, May 1995

**For Pam, Sarah,
and Freddie**
(in that order)

Introduction

In the introduction to my previous book *(Shave the Whales),* I recommended that people sign my name inside the cover and pass it off as an autographed copy. Unfortunately—due to a typo—it appears I went on to promise I would "verify your clam."

Well, needless to say, I have spent the past year explaining to nervous people that clams do not really need verification. So I agreed to put this book out to correct the misperception. I figure you've got enough problems without worrying if your clam is lying to you.

Clams have annoyed me for years. When I became a vegetarian, I used to say that I "wouldn't eat anything with a face," then I would smile with the self-assured look of a man who is both low in cholesterol and incredibly clever. Then my wise-ass friend pointed out that clams don't have faces, so I should eat them. I argued that they have ugly little faces; it's just hard to tell.

But what sometimes gets lost in all this bickering is that if you put an irritant in a clam, and wait long enough, eventually a beautiful pearl will form. Some people say pearls come from oysters, not clams, but these people don't have the credentials in clam verification that I do.

Speaking of pearls, there's still time to join Dogbert's New Ruling Class (DNRC) before he conquers the planet and makes all non-members his slaves. All you have to do is subscribe to the free Dilbert Newsletter.

The frequency of the newsletter is approximately whenever I feel like it. But the e-mail version will be more timely than the paper version.

To subscribe, write:

E-mail: scottadams@aol.com

Snail Mail: Dilbert Newsletter
United Media
Dept. W
200 Park Ave.
New York NY 10166

Scott Adams

7

A SCIENTIST REPORTS THAT LOVE MADE A LAB RAT STUPID.

THE SCIENTIST CAUTIONED THE MEDIA NOT TO DRAW CONCLUSIONS BASED ON ONE RAT.

TIME
LOVE AND S.A.T. SCORES

THE EXPERTS USED TO SAY YOU SHOULD EXERCISE EVERY DAY.

NOW THEY THINK TWENTY MINUTES EVERY OTHER DAY IS JUST AS GOOD.

AMABOR HEALTH CLUB

MY STRATEGY OF FIVE MINUTES A MONTH IS LOOKING PRETTY CLEVER.

HELLO, DILBERT, THIS IS DOCTOR FISHLIPS. I WAS WONDERING IF YOU COULD COME BACK FOR SOME X-RAYS.

X-RAYS? IS THAT STANDARD PROCEDURE A WEEK AFTER AN APPENDECTOMY?

A PATIENT FROM THE PRISON IS MISSING... I'M TOLD THIS ISN'T THE FIRST TIME "TINY TOM" HAS TRIED A BOLD ESCAPE.

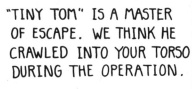

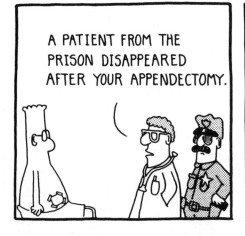

A PATIENT FROM THE PRISON DISAPPEARED AFTER YOUR APPENDECTOMY.

"TINY TOM" IS A MASTER OF ESCAPE. WE THINK HE CRAWLED INTO YOUR TORSO DURING THE OPERATION.

THAT'S STUPID. HOW WOULD HE GET OUT?

EVER SEE THE MOVIE "ALIEN"?

THERE HE IS... TINY TOM THE CONVICT IS CLINGING TO THIS MAN'S PANCREAS.

X-RAY LAB

NOTE:
SOMETIMES IT IS NECESSARY TO SUSPEND DISBELIEF FOR THE PURPOSE OF CREATING COMIC SITUATIONS. PARENTS SHOULD EXPLAIN TO THEIR CHILDREN THAT CONVICTS WILL RARELY, IF EVER, CLING TO ANOTHER PERSON'S PANCREAS.

HO HO, IT APPEARS WE HAVE ALSO LOCATED OUR OWN NURSE WOODMEYER... THE TRAMP!

DOGBERT! I'M HOME AFTER MY SECOND MAJOR SURGERY IN TWO WEEKS!

...SO AFTER THE FIRST OPERATION THEY DISCOVER THAT A TINY CONVICT AND A NURSE HAD HIDDEN INSIDE MY TORSO TO ESCAPE...

BOY...IT SURE IS HARD TO KEEP A MEDICAL STORY INTERESTING.

ZZZZZ

GREAT... NOT ONLY AM I BEING FORCED TO WORK IN THE ACCOUNTING DEPARTMENT, BUT I'M SLOWLY TURNING INTO A TROLL.

BUDGET ERASING UNIT

WAIT A MINUTE...THIS IS THE BUDGET FOR THE ACCOUNTING DEPARTMENT. ITSELF... WHAT HAPPENS IF I ERASE IT?

BOSS!!? BOSS!!?

HELP ME! I'M MELTING! AAAAGH!!

I'VE DECIDED TO JOIN THE ANTI-FUR MOVEMENT.

ISN'T THAT HYPOCRITICAL? YOU WEAR A FUR COAT EVERYDAY.

OH...YEAH, NEVER MIND...

WAIT...

HOW CAN YOU LIVE WITH YOURSELF? HAVE YOU NO CONSCIENCE?

FUR IS MURDER

OH, BIG DEAL... A BUNCH OF MINKS GET BAD HAIRCUTS AND I GET A WARM COAT...

I'LL BET YOU'D MAKE A NICE PAIR OF MITTENS.

I DON'T THINK I REACHED HER.

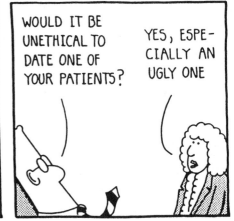

I'D FIX IT MYSELF BUT I KNOW IT TAKES SPECIAL TOOLS...

PLUS I WOULD JUST HAVE TO ORDER A PART... AND I'M PRETTY BUSY...

TAKE TWO OF THESE...

"ENGINEER'S PILLS"?

THEY'LL KNOCK YOU OUT UNTIL I'M GONE.

NOW WE HAVE AN OPPOSING VIEW TO LAST NIGHT'S EDITORIAL ON ANIMAL RIGHTS.

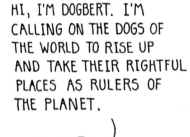

HI, I'M DOGBERT. I'M CALLING ON THE DOGS OF THE WORLD TO RISE UP AND TAKE THEIR RIGHTFUL PLACES AS RULERS OF THE PLANET.

THESE ARE NOT NECESSARILY THE VIEWS OF THIS STATION.

DON'T LISTEN TO HIM. THEY ALWAYS SAY THAT.

TO ME, A WOMAN IS LIKE A FINE BOTTLE OF WINE.

EACH ONE IS FAMILIAR, YET DISTINCTIVE AND SPECIAL.

IN THE WINE OF LIFE, SOME PEOPLE ARE DESTINED TO BE CORK-SNIFFERS.

FOR YEARS MOTHER NATURE HAD BEEN DROPPING HINTS ABOUT THE OZONE PROBLEM.

AAAH... PINE-CONE FRESH LEMON SCENT.

FSSST

FLASH!

THE DIRECT APPROACH WOULD WORK NO BETTER.

IS IT UNSEASONABLY WARM TODAY?

MY PROGRAM PREDICTS THAT TINY HOLES IN THE OZONE COULD LEAD TO ...

FLASH!

ZAP ZAP ZAP

NOW WE'LL NEVER KNOW...

BUT YOU'RE GETTING WARMER.

OKAY, EVERYBODY OFF! LET'S GO, GET OFF!!

MOTHER NATURE?

MOVE ALONG NOW. FIND ANOTHER PLANET.

BUT... BUT...

SHOO! COME BACK WHEN ALL THE PLASTIC IS GONE.

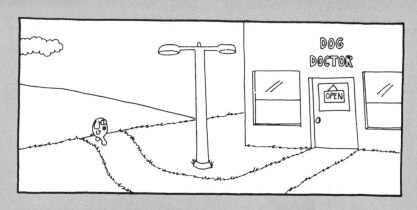

YIKES! DILBERT'S INVENTION IS ALIVE!!

FLASH!

I AM A HOLOGRAPHIC RECORDING OF THE LATE DILBERT, WITH A MESSAGE TO DOGBERT FROM BEYOND THE GRAVE.

...AND MY RECIPE FOR CHILE CON CARNE IS AS FOLLOWS...

UGH...GOSH, WHAT A NIGHTMARE.

BOB, I JUST DREAMED DILBERT WAS KILLED BY DEER, AND ALL HE LEFT ME WAS HIS RECIPE FOR CHILE CON CARNE.

BAD NEWS...

HE'S REALLY DEAD?

AND HIS CHILE CON CARNE STINKS.

NOT MUCH GARBAGE... DID SOMEBODY DIE?

DILBERT WENT TO THE COMPOST PILE IN THE SKY.

BAD TIMING... JUDGING FROM LAST WEEK'S GARBAGE, HE HAD ALMOST FINISHED HIS CLONING MACHINE DESIGN.

I ONLY NOTICE A FEW LINEAR MATH ERRORS.

THIS DESIGN WOULD JUST CREATE A HOLOGRAM AND A BAD CHILE CON CARNE RECIPE.

MAN, YOU SURE KNOW YOUR GARBAGE!

PLEASE, MISTER GARBAGE MAN, HELP US FIX DILBERT'S CLONING DEVICE AND BRING HIM BACK TO LIFE!!

THIS SHOULDN'T BE TOO HARD... STANDARD ANTI-LIGHT RESONANCE FILTERS... YEAH, I THINK I HAVE PARTS IN THE TRUCK.

YOU'RE GOING TO CLONE HIM FROM HIS OWN GARBAGE?

DON'T TELL ANYBODY-- THERE MIGHT BE A STIGMA.

DOGBERT AND THE GARBAGE MAN TRY TO CLONE DILBERT BACK TO LIFE.

PHZUP!

AAAGH! RUN FOR YOUR LIFE!!! IT'S A HIDEOUS, DISGUSTING CREATURE!!!

WOULD YOU CARE FOR A LITTLE "ARM AND HAMMER"?

HI...UH, WHY AM I NAKED AND SITTING IN A GARBAGE CAN?

EITHER YOU WERE KILLED BY WILD DEER AND WE CLONED YOU BACK TO LIFE FROM YOUR OLD GARBAGE... OR...

I HOPE I LIKE THE SECOND CHOICE.

...OR YOU SAVED A LOT OF MONEY ON AN ABOVE-GROUND POOL.

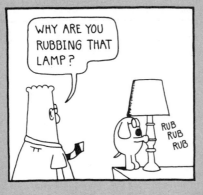

JURY DELIBERATION

I'LL BE THE JURY FOREMAN, SINCE THE REST OF YOU ARE LOSERS.

DID ANYBODY LISTEN TO THE BORING PARTS WITH THE EVIDENCE?

AND NOBODY HAS A COIN?! GEEZ, WHAT'S THIS SYSTEM COMING TO??

HAS THE JURY REACHED A VERDICT?

YES, YOUR HONOR. WE FIND THE DEFENSE ATTORNEY POORLY DRESSED AND OBNOXIOUS. WE SENTENCE HIM TO DEATH.

I DON'T THINK YOU CAN DO THAT.

FURTHERMORE, WE FIND THAT YOUR HONOR LOOKS FETCHING IN A BLACK MUUMUU.

OKAY, THE STAFF MEETING IS OVER. DOES ANYBODY HAVE ANY MEANINGLESS, RAMBLING QUESTIONS?

JOHNSON?

HOW CAN WE WORK AS A TEAM TO ACHIEVE TOTAL QUALITY WITHOUT SACRIFICING CUSTOMER FOCUS?

HOW MANY PEOPLE WOULD LIKE TO SEE ME MAKE JOHNSON FETCH THIS STICK?

NOTICE HOW THE EYES SEEM TO FOLLOW YOU.

WOW, THAT'S A WEIRD EFFECT

IT GETS BETTER.

NEWS

OOH! NICE PILE OF MAIL TODAY!

DILBERT

RESIDENT... RESIDENT... RESIDENT... AHH, DILBERT.

I GET MAIL; THEREFORE I AM.

HOW TO BE A BORING PERSON

OUR FIRST DEMON-STRATION IS CALLED "LISTING THINGS BECAUSE YOU CAN."

I LIKE THE NUMBERS THAT ARE DIVISABLE BY TWO... FOR INSTANCE FOUR... AND TEN... AND SIXTEEN AND EIGHT... AND TWELVE... AND, UH... FORTY... AND TEN, OR DID I ALREADY SAY TEN?

NOW ACT CONFUSED AND START OVER, USING YOUR FINGERS AS IF THAT HELPS.

OKAY, FOUR... AND TEN...

42

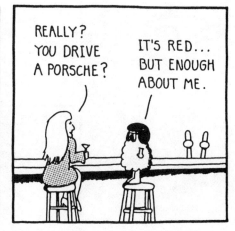

HEY, MISTER, WHY ARE YOU SO GLUM?

I'VE LOST FACE AT MY JOB...

YOU'LL GET OVER IT.

YOU DON'T UNDERSTAND... I'M A PLASTIC SURGEON... I ACTUALLY LOST SOMEBODY'S FACE.

BUMMER

YEAH, I ONCE BUILT AN FM TRANSMITTER FROM OLD TELEVISION PARTS...

THAT'S NOTHING... I BUILT A BROADBAND MULTIPLEXER FROM TUNA CANS AND A LAMP.

... MY FIRST ORBITING SPACE STATION WAS MADE ENTIRELY FROM OLD SOCKS AND VASELINE.

I HATE GOING LAST.

CLUES FROM WOMEN'S HAIR

THIS WOMAN IS SINGLE

THE SAME WOMAN, NOW MARRIED

MARRIED, TWO KIDS

I'M WRITING TO PROTEST THE OBSCENE LYRICS IN OPERA.

IT'S NOT OBSCENE... IT'S A FOREIGN LANGUAGE.

OH... I THOUGHT I WAS JUST LIVING A VERY SHELTERED LIFE.

OPERA SHOULD BE BANNED FROM TELEVISION.

IT MUST BE OBSCENE, OR THEY WOULDN'T HAVE TO SING IT IN A FOREIGN LANGUAGE.

AND WE CAN'T LET CHILDREN THINK IT'S OKAY TO DRESS LIKE VIKINGS AND GO AROUND HOLLERING.

WE GOT A COMPLAINT LETTER FROM A DOG, CHIEF.

TBC

HE CLAIMS TO REPRESENT FIFTY MILLION DOGS WHO OPPOSE THE "OBSCENE" LYRICS OF OUR OPERA BROADCASTS.

OBSCENE? THEY DON'T EVEN SING REAL WORDS.

APPARENTLY IT'S ITALIAN, SIR.

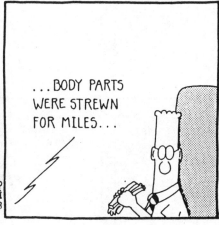

IT IS THE MOST FEARED AND HATED CREATURE ON EARTH	NOT A DINOSAUR 
NOT A RABID DOG 	NOT DONALD TRUMP 
IT IS THE "UGLY SINGLE MALE" 	OTHER MALES FEAR BEING ASSOCIATED WITH HIM 
WOMEN AVOID EYE CONTACT AND FLEE IN HORROR 	ONLY A MAIDEN SACRIFICE CAN END THE HORROR 

I'VE WRITTEN THE ENTIRE ENCYCLOPAEDIA BRITANNICA ON THIS HAIR.

I'LL OPEN A MUSEUM AND CHARGE PEOPLE TO SEE IT.

IT'S KIND OF HARD TO PROVE YOU WROTE ALL THAT ON A HAIR.

I'LL SWEAR ON THIS BIBLE.

THIS NEXT EXHIBIT IS THE PRIDE OF "DOGBERT'S MUSEUM OF THE STRANGE AND AMAZING."

IT LOOKS LIKE A LITTLE PIECE OF CAULIFLOWER.

DAN QUAYLE'S BRAIN

SORRY. WE SHOULD HAVE STOPPED FOR BREAKFAST...

CHOMP CHOMP

WHAT AM I GOING TO TELL MARILYN?

"DOGBERT'S MUSEUM OF THE STRANGE AND AMAZING" IS THE ONLY PLACE YOU CAN FIND...

...A SHIRT WOVEN ENTIRELY FROM A SINGLE THREAD OF TAZMANIAN WOOGAT SILK.

IT LOOKS LIKE THE CHEAP POLYESTER SHIRTS THAT I WEAR.

IN THAT CASE, THIS IS THE GIFT SHOP.

MY MUSEUM IS THE ONLY PLACE YOU CAN SEE THE REMAINS OF D.B. COOPER.

COOPER HIJACKED A JET, DEMANDED MONEY AND A PARACHUTE, THEN JUMPED.

HE LEARNED THAT YOU SHOULD NEVER GET YOUR PARACHUTES FROM THE SAME PEOPLE YOU'RE ROBBING.

THIS EXHIBIT IS THE PRIDE OF "DOGBERT'S MUSEUM OF THE STRANGE AND AMAZING."

THIS IS AN ENGINEER, DEEP IN A COMPUTER-INDUCED TRANCE AND OBLIVIOUS TO HIS ENVIRONMENT.

YOU CAN BOP HIM IN THE BACK OF HIS HEAD WITH WHIFFLE BALLS FOR TEN CENTS A THROW.

GIMME A DOLLAR'S WORTH.

THIS AUTHENTIC CHUNK OF THE BERLIN WALL IS THE LATEST ACQUISITION OF MY MUSEUM.

HEY! YOU MUST THINK WE'RE A COUPLE OF HILLBILLIES. WE SAW A HOLE IN YOUR SIDEWALK IN THAT EXACT SHAPE.

OBVIOUSLY WE HAD TO TRADE A CHUNK OF OUR SIDEWALK TO BERLIN SO WE COULD GET THIS.

APOLOGIZE TO THE DOG, FLOSSIE.

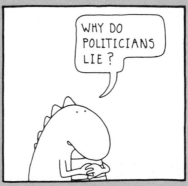

At the "Scientist Anti-Defamation League" we must dispel society's notion that scientists are always male.

Unfortunately, our membership is totally male because all of you joined just to meet women.

Any ideas?

Maybe we could merge with the "Aerobic Instructor Anti-Defamation League."

At the "Scientist Anti-Defamation League"

The bake sale fund raiser is Thursday.

And let's not have a repeat of last year's fiasco when it got so competitive.

Thursday

Put it with the other volcanoes.

Did you notice the indigenous people fleeing in horror?

I'd like to recognize Wilson for working twenty-hour days and making the project a success.

Thanks, but I'm not Wilson. He quit months ago.

Oh...

I've got to stop calling this the Employee Recognition Program.

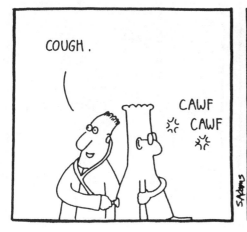

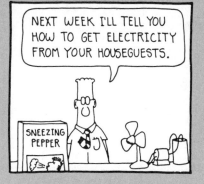

85

WOMEN'S GUIDE TO AVOIDING DILBERT

WEAR STEREO HEADPHONES, LOOK STRAIGHT AHEAD AND OUTRUN HIM.

COMB YOUR HAIR OVER YOUR FACE TO AVOID ACCIDENTAL EYE CONTACT.

TRAVEL IN GROUPS AND MAKE IT CLEAR YOU WILL DISSECT ANY MAN.

DRIVE TO AND FROM SECRET DESTINATIONS IN FAST CARS

MENTION A BOYFRIEND IN EVERY SENTENCE.

NEVER ATTEND A LADIES' NIGHT ACTIVITY.

NEVER GIVE OUT YOUR REAL PHONE NUMBER.

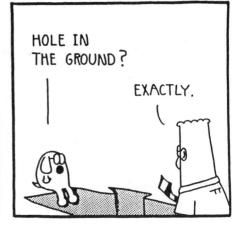

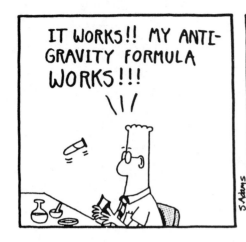

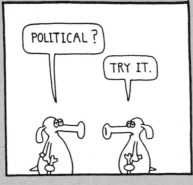

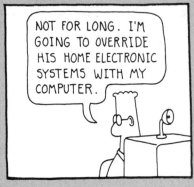

BZZZZZZPP...

I HATE BEING ME.

THE SHREDDER TRIED TO KILL ME.

FIRST, THE COFFEE MACHINE BROKE, RENDERING ME INATTENTIVE ...

WHAT ARE YOU SUGGEST-ING?

I DON'T THINK THE SHREDDER ACTED ALONE.

ON MY RECENT BUSINESS TRIP TO JAPAN, I LEARNED THAT JAPANESE WORKERS DRESS AS THEIR FAVORITE ANIMALS TO BOOST PRODUCTIVITY.

JAPAN

HA HA HA HA HA

OOH-OOH... AND REMEMBER THE TIME WE TOLD THEM WE ALL DO CALISTHENICS?!

ANDROIDS WANT TO BE LIKE HUMANS. TELL ME WHAT HUMANS DO.

MOSTLY, THEY EAT, SLEEP, AND HOPE THEY DON'T DIE.

THAT'S IT?

UNLESS THEY FIND RELIGION... THEN THEY EAT, SLEEP, AND LOOK FORWARD TO DYING.

I HAVE PRACTICED RELIGION FOR ONE DAY AND NOT ATTAINED FULFILLMENT.

THAT'S BECAUSE YOU'RE AN ANDROID. YOU HAVE NO SOUL.

NO SOUL?

WHAT IS A LITTLE CREATURE WITH NO SOUL SUPPOSED TO DO?

WELL, SONNY BONO MARRIED CHER...

AS AN ANDROID, I WONDER HOW HUMANS COPE WITH THE ABSURDITY AND UTTER FUTILITY OF THEIR MEANINGLESS LIVES.

WAS IT SOMETHING I SAID?

**THE SECRETS
OF MEN**

(A GUIDE FOR WOMEN)

WOMEN WONDER WHY MEN SAY DUMB THINGS TO START CONVERSATIONS.

WHY CAN'T MEN TAKE A HINT?

WHY ARE MEN SO THICK?

WHY ARE EXCUSES USELESS?

WHY DON'T MEN UNDERSTAND THE WORD NO?

MEN KNOW WHY THEY ACT LIKE THAT:

... SOMETIMES IT WORKS.

I MADE A SUPER HERO SUIT FOR MYSELF.

WHY?

YOU NEVER KNOW WHEN YOU MIGHT ACCIDENTALLY ACQUIRE SUPER POWERS. IT HAPPENS ALL THE TIME.

THIS WAY, MY IDENTITY CAN REMAIN A SECRET.

I SUDDENLY SEE WHY THAT'S SO IMPORTANT.

I'M TIRED OF WAITING FOR A FREAK ACCIDENT TO BESTOW SUPER POWERS UPON ME.

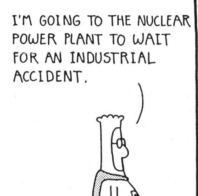

I'M GOING TO THE NUCLEAR POWER PLANT TO WAIT FOR AN INDUSTRIAL ACCIDENT.

KEEP OUT

I SHOULD BE ACQUIRING SUPER POWERS ANY MOMENT FROM THAT RADIOACTIVE BUG BITE.

I WISH I KNEW WHAT KIND OF BUG BIT ME, SO I'D KNOW WHAT POWERS TO EXPECT.

LET'S LOOK IT UP.

"DUNG BEETLE."

BITTEN BY A RADIOACTIVE DUNG BEETLE, DILBERT WAITS TO SEE IF HE WILL ACQUIRE ANY SUPER POWERS.

BUT WHAT KIND OF POWERS COULD YOU GET FROM A BUG WHO LIVES IN DUNG?

FEEL ANYTHING YET?

JUST A WICKED URGE TO ENTER POLITICS.

DO NOT USE IF SEAL IS BROKEN.

GREAT... HOW ARE YOU SUPPOSED TO GET THE PILLS OUT?

PHYSICS MADE EASY

TODAY'S LESSON IS "TIME."

IMAGINE A DONUT, FIRED FROM A CANNON AT THE SPEED OF LIGHT WHILE ROTATING.

TIME IS LIKE THAT, EXCEPT WITHOUT THE CANNON AND THE DONUT.

DOGBERT'S GUIDE TO YOUR TAX DOLLARS

DID YOU EVER WONDER HOW ALL THAT TAX MONEY GETS SPENT?

ROLL THE TAPE.

INVENTING SECRET THINGS.

IT DOESN'T LOOK LIKE MUCH, BUT IT'LL SMART LIKE CRAZY IF YOU SIT ON IT.

SENDING SECRET THINGS INTO SPACE.

MAYBE WE'D BETTER CLASSIFY IT SECRET AND SEND IT INTO SPACE WITH THE OTHER STUFF.

EDUCATION.

SEX WILL KILL YOU, FOOD WILL KILL YOU, SMOKING WILL KILL YOU, ALCOHOL WILL KILL YOU, DRUGS WILL KILL YOU...

ART GRANTS FOR THINGS YOU AREN'T OPEN-MINDED ENOUGH TO APPRECIATE.

I CALL IT "THE BUG I HATED."

ADVANCED HEALTH CARE.

YOU WERE RIGHT, BENSON. X-RAYS AND MICROWAVES ARE NOT THE SAME THING.

PAYING CONGRESS.

OUR RAISES CAME THROUGH!

I THINK I'LL SEND MYSELF A THANK-YOU NOTE!

GIGANTIC CIRCLES CONTINUE TO APPEAR IN BRITISH WHEAT FIELDS.

EXPERTS BELIEVE THE CIRCLES ARE A MESSAGE FROM EXTRA-TERRESTRIALS...

THE MESSAGE HAS BEEN DECIPHERED AS "SURRENDER OR THE WHEAT DIES."

WHAT DO YOU THINK OF THOSE STRANGE CIRCLES FOUND IN BRITISH WHEAT FIELDS?

OBVIOUSLY, MESSAGES FROM HIGHLY INTELLIGENT ALIENS.

IF THEY'RE SO SMART, WHY DO THEY HAVE TO SEND MESSAGES BY STOMPING ON WHEAT?

MAYBE THEY UNDERESTIMATED OUR INTELLIGENCE...

OR NOT.

I'M STANDING AT THE WICKFORD WHEAT FIELDS OUTSIDE OF LONDON, THE SITE OF MYSTERIOUS GIANT CIRCLES, POSSIBLY CAUSED BY ALIENS.

HOW DO YOU FIND THESE CIRCLES OF CRUSHED WHEAT?

MY TEAM OF EXPERTS STARTS AT ONE POINT AND SEARCHES OUTWARD UNTIL...

GOOD LORD! ANOTHER CIRCLE HAS FORMED AROUND US!!

Panel 1: RATBERT, I WANT YOU TO EAT ONE OF DILBERT'S TIES. MAYBE IT WILL HELP SOLVE THE MYSTERY OF WHY THEY ALWAYS CURL UP.

Panel 2: MMM... DELICIOUS, BUT STARCHY... ONE OF THE MORE FULL-BODIED ACCESSORIES I'VE TASTED...

Panel 3: GEEZ... AND THAT WAS ONLY THE PLACEBO NECKTIE.

OIL... CAN...

Panel 4: MISTER GARBAGEMAN, DO YOU KNOW WHY DILBERT'S NECKTIES CURL UP?

Panel 5: IT COULD BE A TANZANIAN NECKTIE SNAKE IN ONE OF ITS CLEVER DISGUISES.

Panel 6: THEY'LL STALK YOU FOR YEARS, THEN SUDDENLY—ACK!!

Panel 7: MAYBE I'LL NEVER SOLVE THE MYSTERY OF WHY DILBERT'S NECKTIES CURL UP.

Panel 8: SOMETIMES, DOGBERT, LIFE PRESENTS US WITH MYSTERIES TO FUEL OUR SENSE OF WONDER... IT STIMULATES US TO REACH BEYOND OURSELVES TO SOMETHING GREATER.

Panel 9: THIS ISN'T ONE OF THOSE TIMES, IS IT?

APPARENTLY NOT.

AS LONG AS YOU'RE HERE, RATBERT, I COULD USE YOUR HELP.

AT YOUR SERVICE!

I'D LIKE YOU TO TEST THE STUFF IN THE FRIDGE AND SEE IF IT'S DANGEROUS.

PUT A QUESTION MARK BY KETCHUP.

I'LL GET US SOME SODAS, RATBERT.

FEEL FREE TO GNAW ON SOME HIGH VOLT- AGE WIRES, OR WHATEVER RATS DO, UNTIL I RETURN.

I DON'T KNOW WHY WE DO THAT, BUT IT SURE WORKS UP A THIRST.

I MUST GET BACK TO THE LAB NOW. BUT PLEASE, NO LONG GOODBYES, OR PART- ING GIFTS, OR FANFARE.

NAY, LET US SIMPLY DRINK IN THE RICHNESS OF THIS BEAUTIFUL YET SORROWFUL MOMENT. TWO FRIENDS WHO...

'BYE

THAT'S WHAT I MEANT TO SAY: "'BYE."